Tender Merci Hope and Healing After Miscarriage

Cindy J. Stagg

ISBN: 1537594621
ISBN-13: 978-1537594620

DEDICATION

Dedicated to my family

ACKNOWLEDGMENTS

There are so many people who work to bring a single book into being. I am thankful for all of them. I owe a huge thank you to my friends Stephenie Larsen and Lori Emery, who each encouraged me and cheered me on while I wrote this book. Without them, the idea for this book would have simply remained that: an idea.

PREFACE

As a society, we don't speak much of miscarriage. It's treated as a private matter, if it's even acknowledged at all. According to The March of Dimes, approximately four million pregnancies are reported every year. Of those, approximately 900,000 to 1,000,000 end in miscarriage. If you count loss that ends before a confirmed positive pregnancy test, some believe that up to 40% of pregnancies end in miscarriage. The truth is, if you haven't personally experienced a miscarriage, then you know someone who has.

So why don't we talk about it? Maybe we're embarrassed. Perhaps we think we did something wrong which caused us to miscarry. Sometimes the grief is too overwhelming. On the other side of that, if you haven't had a miscarriage, then maybe you're not sure what to say when someone you know or love has. Either way, we all find ourselves at a loss for words.

If you have had a miscarriage, then you understand the pain, grief, and loss associated with this event. There are many scientific reasons for miscarriage, and sometimes there is no explanation at all. When a person dies, there are physical, tangible evidences left behind for us to cling to. But when an unborn baby dies, we are left with nothing. Perhaps that is the hardest part of miscarriage. We can only grieve what might have been.

If you are a spiritual person, you might seek comfort in trying to understand God's will for your life. But even then, the process is long and difficult.

Perhaps you have never had a miscarriage yourself, but have a friend or loved one who has. It can be difficult to know what to say or how to help.

Either way, this book is for you. Having a miscarriage is difficult I know. I've had several. It was a trying time in my life. Ultimately, I had more questions than answers. I spent years researching, reading, and studying — in an effort to make sense of it all.

My perspective comes as a member of The Church of Jesus Christ of Latter-day Saints. Whether you believe as I do or not, I think there are findings contained within the pages of this book that will help.

I can tell you, there is hope. You can have peace.

For years, friends encouraged me to write a book about what I found. This is that book. My hope is that you will find comfort in its pages. I hope something will resonate with you that will help you on your journey through the pain and loss of miscarriage; and ultimately the hope of healing your wounds.

LOSS

As a young mother, I remember very clearly coming home from the gym one day, having decided it was time to add a second baby to our family. My first baby was almost two at the time. My husband agreed, and just like that, I was pregnant with baby number two.

Then, just like that, I wasn't pregnant anymore.

I wasn't very far along when I started to spot one day. A little nervous, I called the doctor. He had me come to his office, where he verified I was in fact, having a miscarriage. He said it would be like having an extra-heavy period, gave me some extra-thick pads and sent me on my way. Then, almost as an afterthought, he told me to wait a month before trying again. He seemed pretty nonchalant about the whole thing, so I walked out trying to pretend like everything was okay.

Normal.

Fine.

The truth is, everything was not okay. In fact, I was stunned. I kept asking myself, "What's wrong with me?" I wondered if I had done something that could have caused me to lose this baby.

I went about the rest of that day feeling numb. Nothing felt real. I didn't know how to behave, what to do. The fact that everyone in the doctor's office acted like it was no big deal made me question if I was making the proverbial mountain out of a mole hill.

It was a beautiful spring day in Texas, and the blue bonnets were out in bloom. My original plan for that day was to take my daughter out to a nearby meadow and take pictures of her among the wild flowers.

So I did.

And it was weird.

I wanted to be a cheerful, picture-taking mom. I wanted to be as nonchalant as the doctor had been about the whole thing. But I only felt hollow.

This was so much more than having an extra-heavy period.

There had been a life growing inside of me. Then it was gone. There was no reason for it, and there was nothing I could do about it. There had been so much to look forward to, and suddenly, there was nothing.

Only loss.

That's the thing about a miscarriage. Pregnancy means anticipation. Hope. The future. A sweet little cuddly baby to love for the rest of your life. A baby that is a part of you and your husband. And then, before you even get to say hello, you're saying good-bye.

In many cases, you don't even get to say good-bye.

Doctors and scientists call it tissue. They call it spontaneous abortion. What ugly, hideous words. They're insulting to me as a mother.

I've had seven miscarriages, and I felt the loss of each one of those babies deeply. What some would call tissue, I called my child. I didn't need to wait until I felt those first flutterings in my belly to know and love those babies. They were mine and I loved them the moment I knew I was pregnant. If life is indeed eternal, then I'm sure I loved them even before that moment.

"Tears are all right. They are the price we pay for love, care, and compassion in the world."

- Jeffrey R. Holland

PAIN

As far as doctrine goes, there is very little said, written, or known about miscarriage. Mothers and fathers are left wondering, seeking for guidance and answers to the many questions a miscarriage brings.

Val D. Greenwood, manager of special services, Temple Department, made the following statement on miscarriage and stillbirth: "Though our knowledge of the plan of salvation does not explain why miscarriages and stillbirths take place, nor what the eternal result will be, we can know with confidence that God, who is the father of all spirits, is merciful and just. We can know also that there is hope. Worthy parents can trust in him and know that they and all his spirit children will—one way or another—receive a just reward for their efforts and sacrifice, perhaps in ways that we do not presently comprehend."

May I begin by saying, turn to Heavenly Father first. He wants to answer our prayers. He will send the Holy Ghost to comfort us.

"Wherefore, verily I say unto you that all things unto me are spiritual…"
Doctrine and Covenants 29:34

"I have been many times upon my knees by the overwhelming conviction that I had nowhere else to go."
- Abraham Lincoln

"We truly need Him every hour, whether they be hours of sunshine or of rain."
-President Thomas S. Monson

"We have a responsibility to take our questions to God and struggle with those questions in the process of receiving revelation. Will my personal direction from God be the same as yours? I don't think so. We're individuals. God deals with us as individuals. This is the same God who made not just apples but pears and apricots and persimmons and grapes. He likes diversity. He invented it."
- Chieko N. Okazaki

In her October 2009 General Conference address, Sister Vicki F. Matsumori told the following story:

A Sunbeam teacher wrapped each of her class members one by one in a blanket to teach them how the Spirit feels like the comfort and security of that covering. A visiting mother also heard the lesson.

Many months later the mother thanked the teacher. She told how she had been less active when she accompanied her young daughter to Primary. Several weeks after the lesson, the mother suffered a miscarriage. She was overcome with grief when suddenly she felt a great warmth and peace. It felt like someone had covered her with a warm blanket. She recognized the reassurance of the Spirit and knew that Heavenly Father was aware of her and that He loved her.

["Helping Others Recognize the Whisperings of the Spirit" Vicki F. Matsumori Second Counselor in the Primary General Presidency]

From this short story, I have to ask: why would the mother receive the comfort of the Spirit if it didn't matter to Heavenly Father?

"Blessed are they that mourn: for they shall be comforted."

- Matthew 5:4

It is hard to put into words the feelings I experienced after having a miscarriage. I felt a great loss every single time. 'Grief' seems to be the most fitting word to describe it. 'Grief' holds within its definition loss, sorrow, sadness, anger, guilt, depression. Still, 'grief' is inadequate because the emotion goes deeper than that. There is a weight I felt, as a member of a church whose primary focus is on the family. I wondered what I could have done differently. Why, when trying to fulfill this righteous commandment, I was unable. I felt inadequate, to say the least.

There were several times after losing a baby, that I would find myself lying on the couch, unable and unwilling to get up. My grief was unbearable. I would stay there, staring up at the ceiling, wishing I could disappear into the walls. I didn't think anyone could possibly understand what I was feeling; and I felt utterly alone.

"None of us came to this earth to gain our worth; we brought it with us."
- Sherri Dew

Then one morning I woke up with a tune playing in my head. It was a melody I recognized as a hymn, but to which I did not know the words. As the day went on, the song stayed with me, growing stronger in my mind. It was as if someone was playing a piano right inside my house! Finally, I decided to take the hymn book down from the shelf. The hymn was How Gentle God's Commands. I read through the words, and felt as though Heavenly Father was communicating directly with me through this song. There were two parts especially, that spoke to me:

Come, cast your burdens on the Lord
And trust his constant care.

Why should this anxious load
Press down your weary mind?
Haste to your Heav'nly Father's throne
And sweet refreshment find.
("How Gentle God's Commands," Text by Philip Doddridge)

"Cast thy burden upon the Lord, and He shall sustain thee: he shall never suffer the righteous to be moved."

- Psalms 55:22

As if to prove it to me again, when I walked into the chapel the following Sunday, the organist was playing How Gentle God's Commands as the prelude music. I recognized it as a tender mercy from the Lord. He had reaffirmed my testimony that He knows me and loves me.

"Come unto me, all ye that labour and are heavy laden, and I will give you rest. Take my yoke upon you, and learn of me; for I am meek and lowly in heart: and ye shall find rest unto your souls. For my yoke is easy, and my burden is light."

Matthew 11:28-30

HOPE

Rockwell's Embryo

Dr. P.E. Rockwell gives an account of an experience he once had: "While giving an anesthetic for a ruptured tubal pregnancy at two months, I was handed a very tiny human being. The embryo sac was intact and transparent. Within was a tiny 1/3-inch-long human male swimming extremely vigorously in the bag of waters. He was still attached to the wall by the umbilical cord. This tiny human was perfectly developed with long tapering fingers, feet and toes. His skin was almost transparent, and the delicate arteries and veins were prominent right to the ends of his fingers."

Dr. Rockwell goes on: "The baby was extremely alive and swam about the sac approximately one time every second with a natural, right/left swimmer's stroke. This tiny human did not look at all like the photos and drawings of embryos which we commonly see, nor did he look like the few embryos I've been able to observe since then. The difference was obvious—this one was alive."

He continued: "When the sac was opened, the tiny human immediately lost his life and then took on the appearance of what is accepted as the appearance of an embryo at this state—blunt extremities, etc."

- https://ifonlyforatime.wordpress.com/personality-of-the-fetus/

And the spirit and the body are the soul of man."
-Doctrine and Covenants 88:15

We can assume that a baby growing and developing inside of the womb, who moves and swims and kicks, sucks its thumb, has the hiccups, and responds to sounds - we can assume this baby has a spirit; and we know it has a body. Therefore, according to this scripture the unborn baby must have a soul, thus making it eligible for the resurrection. When we turn to the scriptures, we can find many answers to the questions of miscarriage: Was my baby alive? Will my baby be resurrected? Will I see and know my child again?

"For all old things shall pass away, and all things shall become new, even the heaven and the earth, and all the fulness thereof, both men and beasts, the fowls of the air, and the fishes of the sea;

And not one hair, neither mote, shall be lost, for it is the workmanship of mine hand."

Doctrine and Covenants 29:24-25

"Nothing is more absolutely universal than the resurrection. Every living being will be resurrected. Animal, fowls, fishes, plants, and all forms of life were first created as distinct spirit entities in the preexistence before they were created 'naturally upon the face of the earth.' All forms of life occupy an assigned sphere and play an eternal role in the great plan of creation, redemption, and salvation."

- Bruce R. McConkie

"So we see that the Lord intends to save, not only the earth and the heavens, not only man who dwells upon the earth, but all things which he has created. The animals, the fishes of the sea, the fowls of the air, as well as man, are to be re-created, or renewed, through the resurrection, for they too are living souls." (In Conference Report, Oct. 1928)

- Joseph Fielding Smith

"Are not two sparrows sold for a farthing? and one of them shall not fall on the ground without your Father. But the very hairs of your head are all numbered. Fear ye not therefore, ye are of more value than many sparrows."

- Matthew 10:29-31

If a sparrow holds value in God's eyes, surely these unborn babies have value as well. It does not line up with the doctrines of the church that these babies simply disappear, when all of Heavenly Father's creations are precious to him.

"The Lord takes many away, even in infancy, that they may escape the envy of man, and the sorrows and evils of this present world; they were too pure, too lovely, to live on earth; therefore, if rightly considered, instead of mourning we have reason to rejoice as they are delivered from evil, and we shall soon have them again."

(History of the Church 4:553)

- Joseph Smith

While we can find comfort that we will be reunited with our lost babies one day, the pain and the grief that parents feel after a miscarriage remains here with us now. With miscarriages, there is no funeral, no grave to visit, no closure. Mothers who suffer a miscarriage often grieve in silence. Only one who has experienced the same can truly understand the feelings of her heart.

Some time after my third miscarriage, I attended a youth activity, as part of my duty as a young women's leader. It was my first time in public since losing my baby, and I was still somewhat emotional. I'm not sure why I had gone, other than I felt the need to get on with the normal activity of my life.

I stood near the wall of the gym while the youth played some sort of game. One of the young men's leaders, a friend, came and put his arm around me and said, "I know you've been going through a rough time. I'm sorry."

That small act gave me great comfort - to know that someone else recognized that I was grieving. He may not have understood what my loss felt like, but he took a moment to acknowledge my grief. There was something vastly helpful in this small act. There was no accusation in his tone. There was no prodding or curiosity. It was just a simple *I'm sorry*. Nobody had said those words to me before he did, and nothing had comforted me more.

"Thank you," I said, and decided I was glad I had gone to the church that night.

"That love never changes. … It is there for you when you are sad or happy, discouraged or hopeful. God's love is there for you whether or not you feel you deserve it. It is simply always there."

- President Thomas S. Monson

I would say to mothers who lose a baby through miscarriage, take all the time you need to grieve. Cry, get angry, go for walks, sleep in, let others take care of you, talk it out, pray. Allow yourself to feel all of the emotions that come. Don't hide it or bottle it up as if nothing has happened, because something significant has, indeed happened. You have experienced a great loss.

"Faithfully pursue the time-tested devotional practices that bring the Spirit of the Lord into your life. Seek the counsel of those who hold keys for your spiritual well-being. Ask for and cherish priesthood blessings. Take the sacrament every week, and hold fast to the perfecting promises of the Atonement of Jesus Christ. Believe in miracles. I have seen so many of them come when every other indication would say that hope was lost. Hope is never lost. If those miracles do not come soon or fully or seemingly at all, remember the Savior's own anguished example: if the bitter cup does not pass, drink it and be strong, trusting in happier days ahead."

- Jeffrey R. Holland

To those who wish to help someone who has suffered a miscarriage, I would say this: be kind. We live in a world of social media, where shaming and blaming become all too easy from behind the anonymity of a computer screen. My miscarriages happened before the advent of social media, but even still, there were those who were ready with their accusatory comments.

There was a woman, who under the guise of compassion, suggested that perhaps the reason for all of my miscarriages was that God was punishing me for some unresolved sin in my past. Fortunately for her, I knew better. Not because I have never sinned, but because of the fact that I know God is a God of second (and third and fourth and hundredth) chances. God loves us. But we live in an imperfect world with imperfect knowledge, and sometimes, bad things happen.

Speaking of imperfection, it took me a long time to be able to talk to that woman again. Her words hurt like the serrated blade of a dagger. I needed love; not insensitivity.

If you want to help someone, show compassion. Ask them how they are feeling. Let them know you are there for them. A simple "I'm sorry" is often enough.

I was in the anger phase of grief one evening. We lived in Houston at the time, and the major news story that week was of a woman who had drown her five children in their bathtub. I sat on the floor of my living room, a crumpled heap of tears. The unfairness of the situation was more than I could handle.

At that moment, the phone rang. I was in no mood to talk. I might not have answered, except the caller I.D. indicated it was a good friend. And sometimes, you really need a good friend.

"How are you doing?" She asked.

"Horrible. I'm a mess," I choked out through stifling sobs.

"Not fit for human consumption?" That was her favorite phrase.

I don't remember the rest of the conversation, but by the end, she actually had me laughing. LAUGHING. Me, the angry heap of bitter tears.

I know now what she had done. She had followed the prompting of the spirit. She likely had no idea what to say to me, but she trusted that the Lord would help her. And in doing so, I am the one who was helped.

"The best way to cheer yourself up is to try to cheer somebody else up."

- Mark Twain

I once heard a speaker quote the following verse from the Doctrine and Covenants: "…and I have lifted thee up out of thine afflictions, and have counseled thee, that thou hast been delivered from all thine enemies, and thou hast been delivered from the powers of Satan and from darkness!"

The speaker focused on the phrase "I have lifted thee up out of thine afflictions." He reflected on the fact that Joseph Smith had not been taken out of his afflictions at all. In fact, his enemies raged all about him.

Then, the speaker held up a sheet of paper and said, "If I wanted you to make me an airplane from this paper, I would ask you to make me an airplane OUT of this paper." He pointed out that the paper would be bent and folded and creased until it was made into something that could fly. Likewise, the Lord was lifting Joseph OUT of his afflictions, trying him and bending him until he was made into what the Lord wanted him to be.

The same goes for all of us. The Lord is lifting us OUT of our afflictions. Sometimes we are brought low so that we can be lifted.

"Every trial and experience you have passed through is necessary for your salvation."

- Brigham Young

For our light affliction, which is but for a moment, worketh for us a far more exceeding and eternal weight of glory;

While we look not at the things which are seen, but at the things which are not seen: for the things which are seen are temporal; but the things which are not seen are eternal.

2 Corinthians 4:17-18

Whether we have definitive answers or not concerning the loss of unborn babies through miscarriage, there is one sure thing that remains constant: the infinite Atonement of Jesus Christ. At the end of the day, after we have shed our tears, sought answers through prayer and scripture study, we still have the Atonement. Infinite in its scope, the Savior has already paid the price to make up for all of our losses, all of our suffering, and all of our pain. No matter how deep our hurting, the Atonement reaches out and takes it, saving us from eternal despair.

"In striving for some peace and understanding in these difficult matters, it is crucial to remember that we are living—and chose to live—in a fallen world where for divine purposes our pursuit of godliness will be tested and tried again and again. Of greatest assurance in God's plan is that a Savior was promised, a Redeemer, who through our faith in Him would lift us triumphantly over those tests and trials, even though the cost to do so would be unfathomable for both the Father who sent Him and the Son who came. It is only an appreciation of this divine love that will make our own lesser suffering first bearable, then understandable, and finally redemptive."
- Jeffrey R. Holland

"Those who move forward with a happy spirit will find that things always work out."
- Gordon B. Hinckley

I can honestly say that the pain of miscarriage eases. I think about my unborn babies often; they have been woven into the fabric of my very existence - but the grief and sadness diminish. Each miscarriage proved to be some of the most challenging times in my life, but they were also some of the most tender. I felt the love and comfort of my Heavenly Father more deeply and tangibly than at any other time. I felt as Lehi said, "encircled about eternally in the arms of His love."

"All your losses will be made up to you in the resurrection, provided you continue faithful. By the vision of the Almighty I have seen it." (History of the Church 5:362)

- Joseph Smith

ABOUT THE AUTHOR

Cindy J. Stagg is a writer, a speaker, and storytelling consultant. She lives in the mountain tops of Utah with her husband and two children, where you'll very often find her paddle boarding on one of the many lakes near her home.

PLEASE LEAVE A REVIEW

If you enjoyed reading this book, please consider leaving a review on Amazon. I would love to hear from you!

CONTACT ME

thebrightwords1@gmail.com

Made in the USA
Monee, IL
05 February 2021